The Art Of Social Media Marketing

Noorani, Faizal

CIEL ENTERPRISES

The Art Of Social Media Marketing

LEGAL NOTICE

About The Author:

Noorani, Faizal is an upcoming author and a content writer from **Mumbai (India).** He is more into digital and technological writings. He being from the media and broadcasting background he has always been inclined more towards technology and technical areas.

Noorani, Faizal took up writing as a hobby and not as a profession. Hence he loves writing about the work he is into.

You can follow him at:

Twitter: https://twitter.com/cielenter

Facebook: https://www.facebook.com/cielenterp

Visit: https://cielenterprises.gq

We all know how big social media is.
Social media is the fastest growing trend in the history of the world.

This sector has grown faster than the Internet itself.

With the rapid expansion of technology we can communicate with people at the other end of the world.

Over the years, social media has changed the way that we communicate, share information, and play games over the internet and other digital platforms. At the same time Social media has also helped businesses connect with existing customers while introducing new consumers to their products and services. Social Media has not just affected business but also has affected our personal lives.

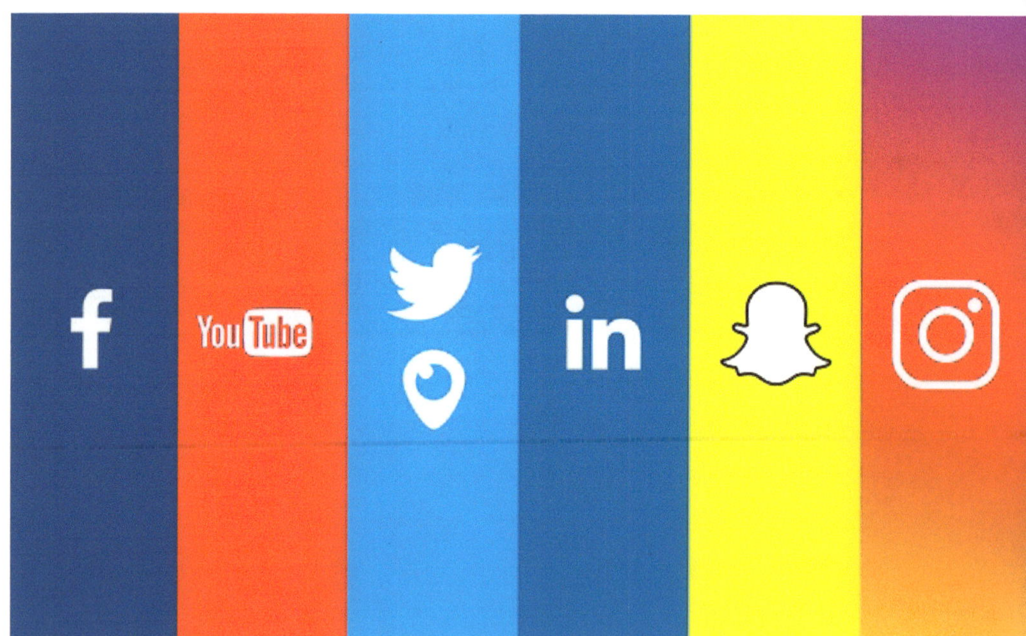

Nomophobia is the fear of not being near your mobile phone.

With such widespread use, social media presents an incredible marketing opportunity.

In this social media marketing guide, I'm going to walk you through few most popular platforms.

I'll give you an overview of each one, show you how to build a successful social media strategy for them, and point you to some of the best ways to use them in your business.

Defining Social Media

Social Media is something that allows websites and computer programs to people to communicate and share information on the internet using a computer or mobile phone.

Social media marketing is the process of creating content that you have tailored to the context of each individual social media platform in order to drive user engagement and sharing.

You gaining traffic is only the result of social media marketing. What do you do to get that result? Create content that works well on each platform.

Every social media platform are different. Like for some platform creating a content in a video script does well like – YOUTUBE. Whereas some platforms you need images as their content like – PINTEREST & INSTAGRAM, a few need writing – blogs and articles. Hence every social media is different but servers the same.

REACHING OUT TO MILLIONS OF PEOPLE OUT THERE!

The more your content is exciting the more people will reach and the more it will be shared. As it is always said **"Content is the King".**

Everyone wants their content to go viral and be famous.

But, to do that, the content must be engaging so that people want to share it. Your content must be so good that it makes the user want to tell all of his or her friends about it.

Hence if you do not create good content you will not have shares, no viral content, and no traffic back to your site.

As per **Wikipedia** alone there are over 200 social media platforms available.

This great graphic called **"The Conversation Prism"** gives a good overview.

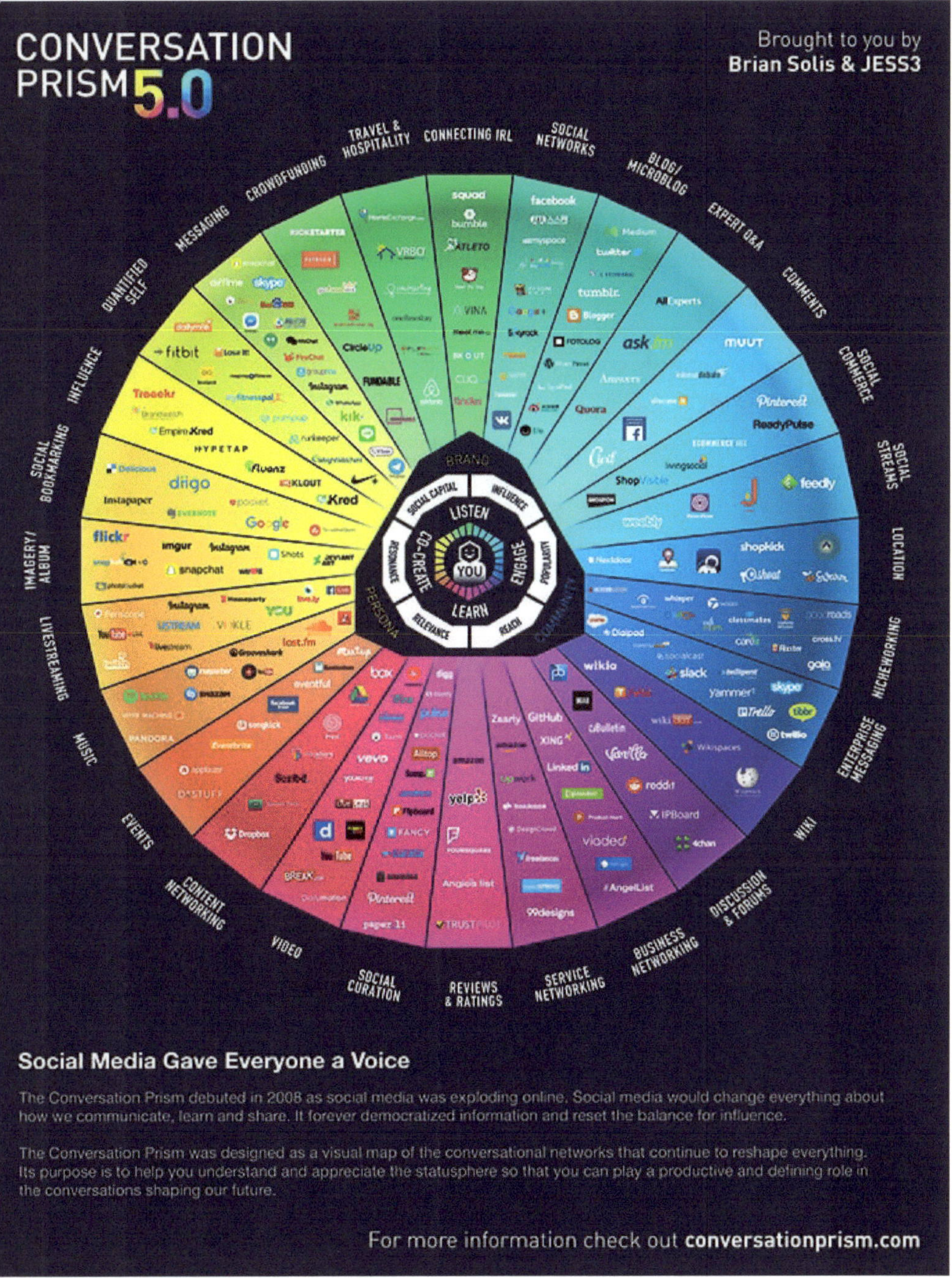

The world of social media is changing incredibly fast. There are new things and ways to communicate through the social media platforms.

Let's look at some key social media terms.

Content: Content is whatever you are posting. It can be a Facebook status update, a photo on Instagram, a tweet, something to pin on a board on Pinterest, and so on.

As mentioned earlier content can be in different forms which may serve different platforms. Social media can give you the opportunity to improve your brand identity, reach new customers, and communicate with potential customers. Using these platforms in the right way.

Hashtags: By now, they're a very common form that people use to add meta information on almost all social media channels. Twitter, Facebook, Instagram, and Pinterest all use hashtags to let you describe the topic of your content or mark it as part of current trends.

Shares: Shares are all that matters on social media.

You would want people to share your stories, experiences, videos, articles or even images and hence share plays a very important role in Social Media. You should always give an option to the visitor of your website to share your content further ahead.

A great tool to measure shares and the overall impact of content is **BuzzSumo**:

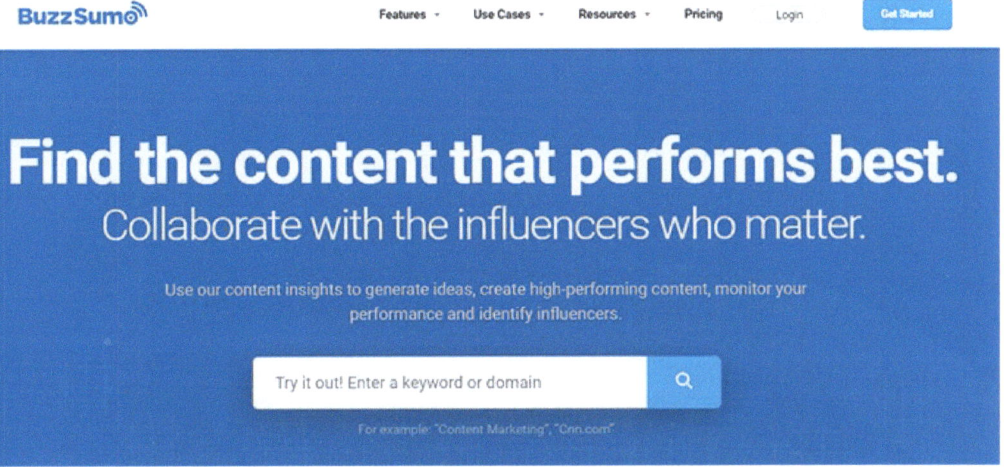

Engagement: This is a general term that means that people interact with the content that you produce. It can be a like, a recommend, a comment, or a share. All of these are good, but the shares are where it's works the best.

The social media world changes faster than any other online space.

It keeps you on your toes. You cannot avoid staying behind the social media.

Organic reach vs Paid reach

Even today there are misconceptions on **Organic reach vs Paid reach.** Just for an intro - **Paid Search** results are ones for which you will pay money. **Organic Search** results are free results. Organic listings are free of cost. Success in organic search completely dependent upon your staying on top of "on page" content on your site. Paid search can essentially guarantee (for a price, of course) placement. It's you who decides how much to spend for Paid Search Campaign to get a constant flow of traffic. Most importantly you are the decision maker as to how much you would like to spend on the campaign.

Paid listings are shown in a shaded area at the top of the page. Because paid results are visible above or in addition to organic results. A Paid listing is often shaded with background color, outlines, or other visual identifiers. Once upon a time, a social media user could post compelling content and easily grow their social media following.

But today, that's not so much the case now days.

Most social media platforms are making it increasingly difficult to build an organic following. Here's why. As the ability for organic superstars to shine goes down, something else goes up.

Every social media platform makes it more difficult for users to grow their own organic platform so that businesses spend more money on advertisements. And hence they can profit out of them.

We should not forget that: **Social media platforms are businesses.**

Facebook, Instagram, Twitter, and every single other social media space wants to make money.

And they do that by connecting you with paying customers. But it's you who will keep a watch on what platform is better and benefits your business. You cannot just put in your money and expect results.

As organic reach becomes more difficult, businesses have to pay for traffic to get generated at their website or their sales page.

The more those social media algorithms prioritize advertisements, the more those businesses are willing to pay.

This is why social media ad spend is on the way up. Advertising budgets for social media tripled from 2014 to 2018. And it seems it will go on a rise further.

It makes sense when you find out that social media companies make practically all of their money from advertisements.

Average Revenue per User (ARPU)

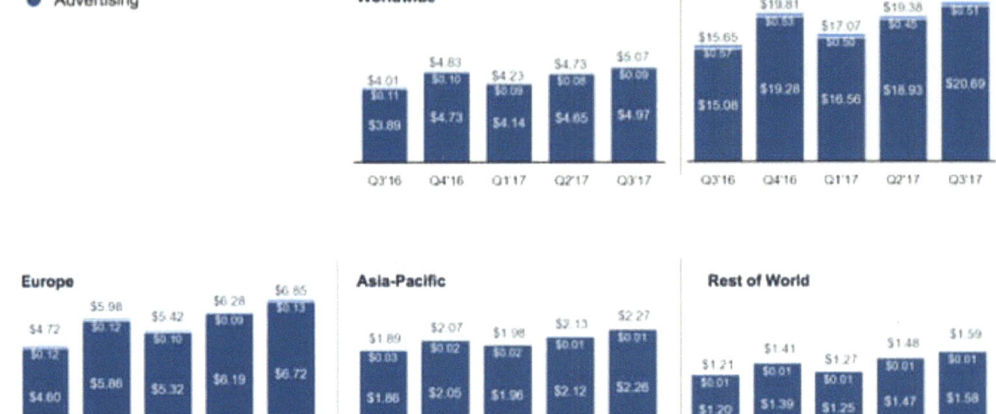

In other words, social media is only free for users because advertisers are paying loads of money to reach those users.

If you want to reach mass audience, you have to pay. Fortunately, if you choose the right social media platform for your business to invest money into, that won't be too big of a problem. Most social media sites still have very reasonable advertising costs, particularly if you have thought through your advertisements well.

As mentioned earlier as the new technologies come in we figure out how to reach more and more people efficiently. And that trend isn't slowing down. As new ways of communicating, reaching customers, and pulling leads develop, so do strategies that are equally innovative.

ake, for instance, **cart abandonment emails.** Once, the only place to send and
eceive cart abandonment messages was through email.

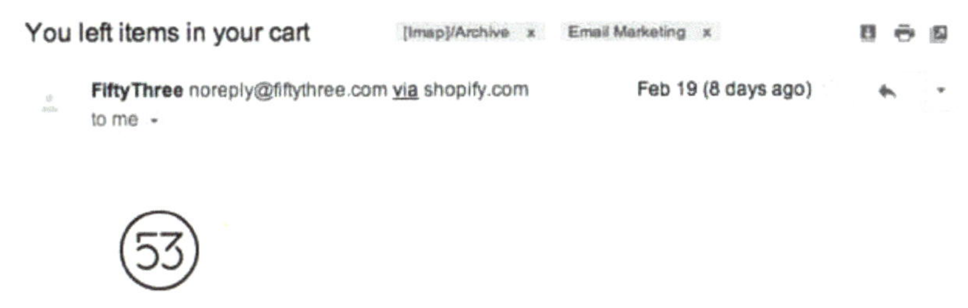

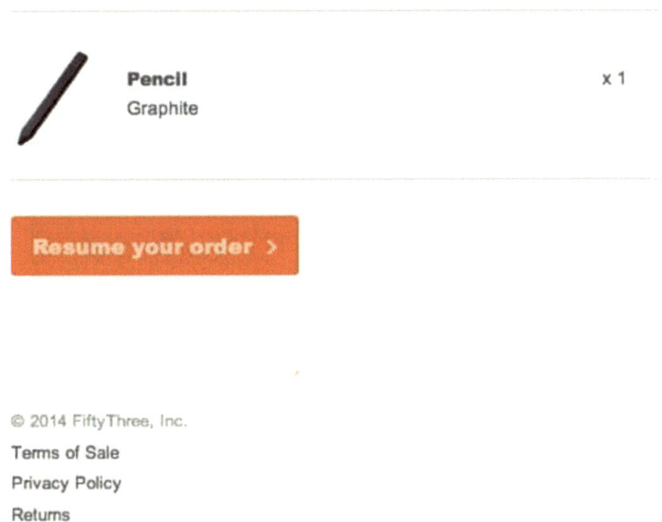

But as mentioned there are also other platforms which have caught up with the promotions and advertising on their platforms.

As more and more social media sites find their footing, expect the merging of different marketing channels to happen even more than it already has.

Tools are merging

But it's not just the channels that are merging. The tools we use are also merging.

Take **MailChimp**, for example.

With MailChimp, email marketing software, users can create Facebook Ads natively from their MailChimp accounts.

They can do so to target their email subscribers or create a lookalike audience from their current subscribers.

The more that this happens between social media platforms and SaaS companies, the easier time you'll have marketing to your target audience.

This merging of online tools is a good thing for your business.

Facebook

History: Like the movie name suggests, this is the social network. When Mark Zuckerberg and his co-founders created the site in a Boston dorm room in 2004, they only made it accessible to Harvard students. But they quickly realized the site's potential. After expanding to Ivy League colleges and a few others, they opened Facebook to everyone in 2006.

Now, it's the biggest social media platform out there. It offers marketers the most data and the most targeted ads.

With Facebook Ads, you can target management executives, startup companies, and many other individuals who promote and sell their services and products or who want to reach masses.

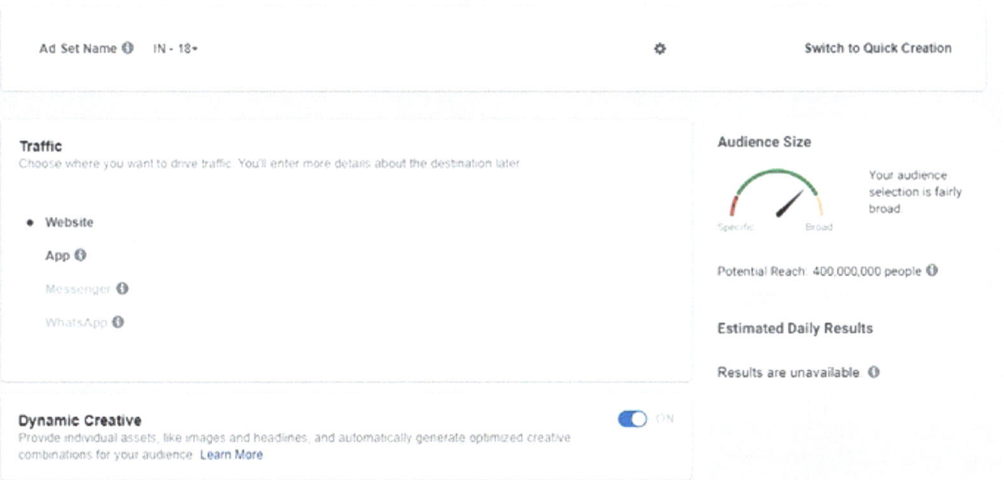

Context: Facebook gives you a lot of freedom when it comes to content. Images, videos, and text posts all work.

For example, instead of just posting a link to a YouTube video, upload the video to Facebook's own platform. If you want to redirect people to a giveaway or landing page, publish it as a tab inside your fan page.

Your aim is to try to keep your user on the platform as long as possible.

Facebook Business Manager

If you want to advertise on Facebook, the first thing you need to know about is the **Facebook Business Manager** tool.

This as a hub for managing your advertisements, pages, and people.

It's free and quite simple to use.

Go to the landing page for the Facebook Business Manager. Click "Create Account" in the top right-hand corner.

Arc and Business Manager Overview

Then, you'll see this overlay come up. Simply enter your business name and click "Continue."

Business Manager Overview

Now enter your name and your business email, and then click "Finish."

You'll now see your Business Manager dashboard. Feel free to browse around to get a feel for its capabilities.

This tool is an absolute must for anyone who's serious about advertising and marketing on Facebook. It will give you a single place to worry about your marketing performance rather than having to jump from tab to tab.

Facebook Advertising options

The best part about Facebook is the specificity with which you can target your ideal customer.

You can choose to target people based on their demographic, device, age, interests, and a load of other characteristics.

The first thing you'll get to choose when creating a Facebook advertising campaign is the goal of your campaign.

Do you want to drive traffic to your website, drive conversions, promote your Facebook Page, get engagement on your post, or something else?

Just select the one you want.

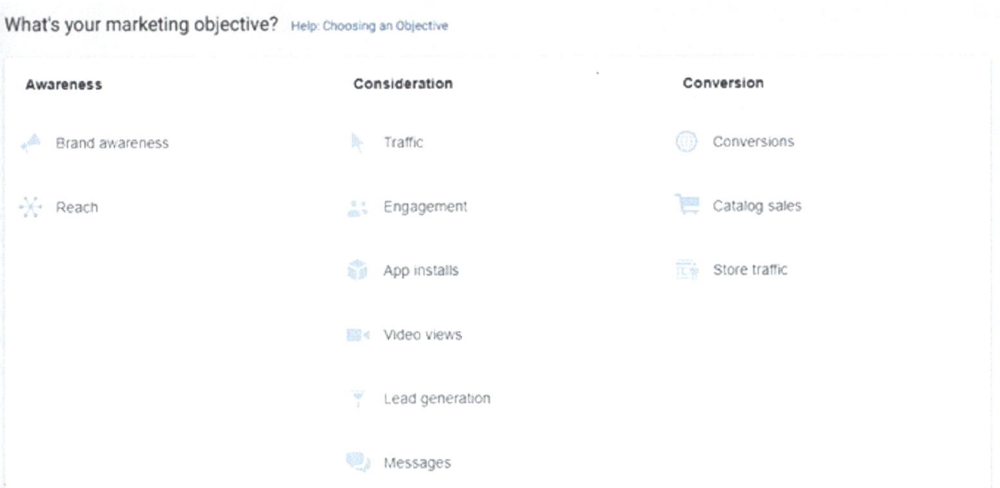

Then, you'll also get to choose your audience based on their location, age, gender, language, interests, behaviors, and connections.

Finally, you'll be able to select the devices you want to target and where you want your ads to show up.

Facebook recommends using auto ad placement, but if you disagree, you can just as easily decide where you want your ads to go and what device you want them to target.

Many social media platforms will make all these decisions for you. But Facebook puts you in the driver's seat because they know you'll likely do the best job of finding your ideal customers.

You, after all, know your target market best.

Fortunately, when you find your perfect audience, you can leverage it.

Facebook allows you to create lookalike audiences.

The best part is that you can also integrate Instagram with it.

Instagram integration

Did you know that when you create an ad on Facebook, you can also run that ad on Instagram by clicking a single button?

That's right. It takes you no extra work.

You can simply click the Instagram ad placement button and select "Feed," "Stories," or both.

If your ad is highly visual and your target market is younger people, then you might want to consider using this automatic integration.

It will expand your reach with no extra work.

Facebook Live

People love Facebook live. Facebook live has now become more often popular in recent times. There are companies who would put their webinar, DIY, or even launch a product via Facebook Live.

There's just something about live video that makes it more appealing.

Facebook Live makes people more connected!

And since it's still early in its development, live video isn't crowded yet. That means that it's ripe for the taking.

Instagram

Within three months of releasing Instagram in the app store, it had reached 1 million users.

Their growth was entirely organic. The app was so good that it dominated the app store charts for months..

The way the app works is almost entirely the same. People post pics, tag friends, insert hashtags, and double tap to show they like what others share.

Facebook acquired Instagram in 2012, only 24 months after they started, for a whopping $1 billion. And in 2015, they rolled out the use of ads for everyone.

Instagram is and was always about pictures. Out of all of the big networks, Instagram has the highest engagement rate.

Since liking is so easy (you just double tap on a picture as you scroll through your feed), people tend to do it more on Instagram than on Twitter or Facebook.

But like Facebook you cannot have lengthy videos, You can release 15-second videos on Instagram, but very few accounts do that successfully. People tend to like and comment more on pictures. However, posting video on Instagram can certainly work, too. You can make a video of your brand, service or product and publish it over the Instagram platform.

But, if I were to start a new Instagram account from scratch, I'd focus entirely on pictures. Here are a few categories that work well:

Inspiring quotes

Put in images with Inspiring quotes. Of course, you must also make use of hashtags, give a call-to-action with each photo, and make sure that you're using your bio right (it's your only chance to link back to your site).

Instagram is winning big.

It's no surprise, then, that **72%** of brands participate in influencer marketing.

Instagram Stories is a feature that lets users create a coherent series of pictures, videos, or gifs.

YouTube

This social network has changed the way we consume video since it has made it easy (streaming is super-fast) and free, and it gives us a way to express our opinions instantly.

Users watch about one billion hours of video on YouTube every single day. That's 114,000 years of time!

About ten years ago, no one could make living playing video games. But now people like **Daniel aka Dantdm** and **Felix Kjellberg, aka PewDiePie,** is one of the biggest earners on the platform, having made 124 million dollars since 2010.

About 40 million people watch his every move with the joystick, and he has even released his own game.

Thanks to YouTube, people can now build a nice, small business teaching things, sharing makeup tutorials, doing funny pranks, or sharing their athletic abilities (or lack thereof).

For example, you could turn your blog posts into video tutorials.

There are two ways to succeed on YouTube. You can either **entertain or teach.**

There is no limit to how long your videos can be, and people have published entire courses in the form of a single, 3-hour video.

Sure, since YouTube is video-based, it requires a bit of videography knowledge and a bit of the right equipment. But already, tons of different online phenomena are DIY-ing their way to becoming YouTube sensations.

Even your iPhone will do. Post-production and editing. It's not just video filming that the DIYers are taking over. It's also post-production and editing.

In fact, every year it seems, new tools come out that allow people like you to edit your video content with ease.

For editing your own video content for YouTube, consider WeVideo. It's is free and easy to use.

With it, you can layer content, cut content, and even add new graphics.

YouTube Video ads

Finally, you might want to consider using video ads on YouTube

Depending on the type of ad you choose to use, viewers will either be able to skip your ad after a few seconds or YouTube will make them watch the entire thing. Naturally, different strategies will work for different businesses.

Don't be afraid to try different things. A/B test to see what works best and what doesn't work at all.

In the end, your advertisement on YouTube will only be as good as your determination to find out what works.

LinkedIn

LinkedIn is older than Facebook. Reid Hoffman, one of the early members of PayPal, founded it in 2002.

But initial growth was slow. LinkedIn's growth never exploded as much as Facebook's, but they've been around for 15 years and have grown to over 467 million members.

The strategy that got them some traction was focusing on what worked well. For example, they gave a lot of attention to their homepage, which accounted for 40% of their sign-ups.

What they always had going for them was being profitable very early. Thanks to premium subscriptions, a paid job board, and a few other freemium options, they were making money after only three years of being in business. LinkedIn started as a simple job search tool and today it had grown way beyond it.

Now days we use LinkedIn for research, marketing and not just as a job search tool.

According to one study, 50% of B2B buyers use LinkedIn in their purchase decisions. Another 70% of professionals viewed LinkedIn as a trustworthy source of content.

Users are very engaged on LinkedIn.

Linkedin is more than simply a way to make business connections. Many use LinkedIn to…

- **Publish thought leadership content**
- **People engage with like-minded communities and groups**
- **Search organization for new job opening**

LinkedIn, it's all about being professional. The casual writing style that's used to make some blogs, including my own, so popular, doesn't work as well on LinkedIn. People are there for one thing only: business.

They want to learn about what's new in their industries, who's hiring, who's firing, and how to optimize their performance at work.

LinkedIn Groups

If you're familiar with Facebook Groups, then LinkedIn Groups shouldn't stretch your imagination too far.

Just think of Facebook Groups but for business people.

Basically, LinkedIn Groups are a place for like-minded professionals to gather and discuss topics of interest or establish their expertise.

After all, the more people that believe your business knows what it's talking about, the more people who will work with you in the future.

LinkedIn Advertising

As with all social media platforms, you can also use LinkedIn to run your advertisements. And if your business falls into the B2B category, LinkedIn might just be the best place for your advertisements. In fact, marketers rate LinkedIn as the most effective social media platform for B2B companies.

Since people on LinkedIn are there to talk business, they also don't mind interacting with businesses.

That means that your business can get some serious attention on the platform if you play your cards right.

Snapchat

Snapchat has about 178 million daily active users. While the majority of those are girls (about 70%), the boys who share on the platform have one thing in common: They're young.

1% of the users are under 34 years old. The hacks and spam and naked selfie scandals might easily distract the average adult from the fact that this is one serious platform for marketers.

Though the app has only been around for a few years (since September of 2011), it is already worth around $33 billion (though there is some disagreement amongst sources).

If your products are targeting 14-year-old girls and you're not on Snapchat, you are doing something wrong. Since all images and videos disappear after 10 seconds max, the context suggests that all content on the platform is fleeting and short-lived.

For example, you could give your audience access to a live event. If you're giving a talk at a conference, take a few snaps when you're on stage and share them with your followers.

Snapchat is all about sharing those precious moments that we all have so few of in life, so make sure that you use it for just that.

A product catering to youngsters should be published on **Snapchat**, because that's where you will find youngsters.

Pinterest

Pinterest is the number one social media platform for marketers who want to target women. 81% of their 150 million monthly active users are female. You can think of the site as a giant digital scrapbook.

Between their closed launch in 2010 and 2012, you needed an invitation to get on the platform, so it's only been open to the public for five years. Nevertheless, the leads you acquire from Pinterest are high-quality.

Even though Pinterest doesn't yet make any serious money except for a few ads for famous brands, they are definitely one of the top ten most influential social platforms right now.

Pinterest is all about user-generated content, so it's good to be personal.

Due to the nature of the pin boards, Pinterest is also one of the only platforms where images look best when you display them vertically. Keep in mind that your pics need special formatting to look good on Pinterest.

To know more how you can master Pinterest I have written a separate article **here**.

Quora

Two former Facebook employees created it in 2009 and made it public in 2010. They thought that **Q&A** was one of the great formats of the Internet, but up to that point, no one had built a solid platform for it.

It turned out that they were right. With a comparatively low $80 million in funding so far, they have built Quora up to over 190 million users in eight years.

Users can ask questions, and if they're popular, users can re-ask them. Users can also up vote answers to make sure that quality answers show up first.

Quora is one of the platforms that I believe all online entrepreneurs should devote at least a small bit of time to. It's basically a question and answer forum where people can go and ask or answer on any given topic. Quora tends to rank well on Google, too. So, Quora gives you more bangs when it comes to time spent on increasing traffic. To use Quora all you need to do is answer questions in a strategic way. You simply need to sign up for an account and start engaging with topics that interest you.

People have built entire platforms from answering questions on Quora, and some answers boast more than 1 million views.

Try to give answers that will still be valid in a year or two or even five. Some of the most popular Quora answers came from years ago.

You can double your benefit from Quora if you use it to come up with content. For example, you could write a blog post that gives a very detailed answer to a popular question.

This will also help you build a reputation as an expert on your topic. If someone likes an answer that they read from you, they'll often browse through the other answers that you've given

Hence now you understand how important **SOCIAL MEDIA MARKETING** is. I have covered only a few of them just to give a glimpse how vast the platform is. So if you are into business you cannot avoid Social Media Platform in anyways. Because this is where you will find your Potential Customers.

With this we come to an end of this topic…

I hope you have enjoyed reading and have gained something out of it. Do let me know on what other topics you would like to read.

I would appreciate if you could leave a review on the topic, this will help me write more refined content.

Do share the content on your social media..

Till then Happy Reading…

Noorani, Faizal

You may be interested in my other titles you may check them out here:

- **ClickBank Your Gateway To Online Business: A Passive Income Guide For 2020**
- **An Introduction To Google Algorithm**
- **All You Need To Know About Email Marketing**
- **Secret To Successful Affiliate Marketing 2020**
- **Proven Ways To Drive Traffic To Your Blog Or Your Website**
- **Tips on INCREASING Sales on Instagram**
- **Guide To Search Engine Optimization - 2019**
- **A Guide To Digital Marketing For Beginners**
- **Advanced Guide To Digital Marketing**
- **The Importance Of Customer Loyalty**

Available Now On

www.ingramcontent.com/pod-product-compliance
Lightning Source LLC
Chambersburg PA
CBHW040319240726
48664CB00006B/1554